MY Heart
FULL OF ALL

WRITTEN BY:

JIA SHAO

This book is dedicated to all children.
You are the best of this whole wide world.

This book belongs to

_____

Mommy, Mommy, can we have a fashion show?

I sprinkled the catwalk with glitter and glow.

All the models are ready inside my toy box.
I'll take my doll and you can take Mrs. Fox.

You and Daddy made a perfect mix such as mine.
So, just as I am, I want my dolls to shine.

The lights are on the stage in the shape of a heart.
The audience is impatient, so soon we should start.

First, I will put my doll
on the chair.

How will I tame and style her great hair?

Her hair is like mine, as you can see.
So I'll make her two buns, as you made for me.

This hairstyle is super cool and a brand new fad.
I'm so glad I inherited it from my funny dad.

I love Daddy's smile and his brightening glance.
Together we create fun songs while we dance.

His culture is lovely, rich and full of art.
I'm lucky to have this part in my heart.

Let's choose a dress from
the ones we have here.

I like most the one you wore for Chinese New Year.

Remember when we watched the dragons dance all night, and decorated the walls all red and so bright?

I put a lot of dumplings in my little tummy. I remember how they were so tasty and yummy.

The red buttons are perfect on this dress dyed blue.

I'm happy you let me meet this side of you.

And what about the shoes? They must be something chic.

When we were in the Netherlands, I saw something unique.

Everyone wore clogs to celebrate King's Day;
clogs in so many colors: green, yellow, purple and gray.

It was the best day ever I spent with a smile.
I realized that orange might be my fashion style.

Now I will add a sweet dot tinted red.
I often saw my Aunt wear it on her forehead.

Aunt's culture is amazing in so many ways.
She took me to an Indian wedding that lasted three days.

One last touch and my doll will be ready to go.
Her henna patterns will be highlight of our show.

Ta-dah!
Look, Mommy, she's perfect
with a little bit of all.
All the cultures look so great
on my doll.

Now we'll serve sweet pudding that you make the best.
The mango tastes perfect for our mixed-race fest.

I love knowing languages I learned from my cousins:
Grandmas, aunts, grandpas, and uncles in the dozens.

I love our family coming from all over the world.

I love my eyes a bit slanted
and that my hair can be
straight, braided, or curled.

I love hearing about their cultures and traditions too.

They all have something in common,
good hearts like me and you.

Just one more thing, I'd like to say with glee.
I'm proud to carry a part of you both inside me.

I'm so glad I don't have to choose either side.
I'm both of my parents! I speak this with pride.

Are you ready? The fashion show is starting soon.
Take your seats, because it'll last until noon.

Let's sprinkle the runway with red roses in bloom.
The whole world has come into my little room.

What's your favorite cultural festival?

All cultures are AMAZING!

_____

Can you write "Hello" in different languages?

All languages are AMAZING!

_____

Can you draw a henna pattern?

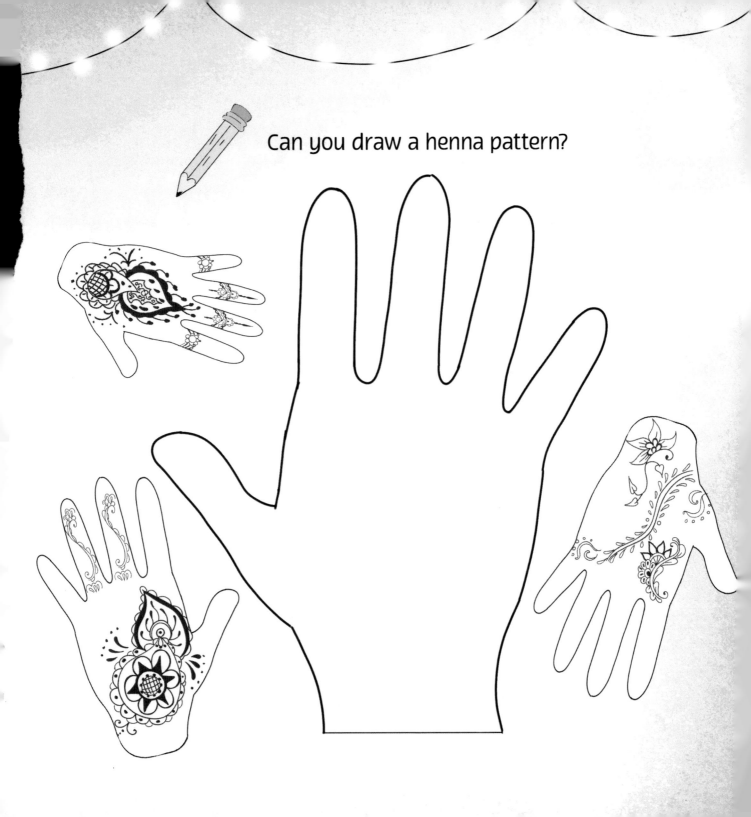

Made in the USA
Coppell, TX
17 March 2024

30204310R00024